MARILYN
THE MOTHER, WIFE, AND TEACHER

Anatoly Bezkorovainy

Author's Tranquility Press
Marietta, Georgia

Anatoly Bezkorovainy /Author's Tranquility Press
2706 Station Club Drive SW
Marietta, Ga 30060
www.authorstranquilitypress.com

This is a work of nonfiction.

Ordering Information:
Quantity sales. Special discounts are available on quantity purchases by corporations, associations, and others. For details, contact the "Special Sales Department" at the address above.

Hardback: 9781956480504
Paperback: 978-1-956480-29-0
eBook: 978-1-956480-30-6

<u>P R E F A C E</u>

When I turned 80 some time ago, I noticed that my memory was gradually losing its former events much more rapidly than in the past. Many past events were gradually disappearing from my mind, which losses l did not experience with any great joy. And such losses did not easily come back, which I missed miserably. I looked to remember my past, and I was beginning to lose it. So, what could I do? Many people had started diaries sometime in their youth, others in their Middle Ages... But when they die, their diaries get soon lost since their descendants may not be particularly interested in their ancestors' histories. Others, however, may write novels or stories about tales in their diaries, yet others may even publish them. But these latter types are very uncommon. So, I decided to join these uncommon types and write a story about my wife and me before I die or forget all about our lives. Having a written or even printed record of one's love affair and marriage will not be lost easily and most likely will remain in one's brain until the end of one's life.

I was now and then recalling a life of a colleague of mine of fond memory, whose biography could have been a good story, but because of a love affair, it turned out less successful than it could have been. I will briefly relate this story because a very few times did I have similar feelings in my lifetime, though I did not follow them, and they soon disappeared thereafter, thanks be to God. Here goes: Dr. X was an Australian who had received his doctorate in biochemistry. After a post-doctorate job, he was hired by my Biochemistry Department chairman as Assistant Professor, presumably to help me handle our 120 medical student Biochemistry course, of which I was the course director. I don't know why my boss hired him; he didn't ask me anything about that matter, I had never complained about my work being too hard, nor could I be fired since my title was already Associate Professor and I had tenure, even if my boss wanted to. But to get some help, I did not mind, and my boss asked me to help the new Assistant Professor start his career, including doing research. So I invited him to our research group, and we published a nice group of research papers on transferrin and other topics of my interest.

He was a decent researcher, and eventually, he was able to get his own grants and run his own research projects. However, I retained my job as a course director for the medical biochemistry course, which our new Assistant Professor apparently wanted to be a member of. Eventually, I got notice that my colleague was appointed Assistant Dean of the medical school. That job lasted for a year; he got another "promotion" at the Dean's office and stopped teaching biochemistry. I was promoted to full professor with basically the same jobs, giving a couple of lectures a year only.

Eventually, my colleague got a national job, I believe, with an organization that makes national medical exams. Then I lost knowledge of his career, but eventually, I saw signs on the Illinois highways with Dr. X picture advertising his real estate sales office. He became a real estate sales/buying agent. His private life was also coming along; he came to America with a wife and two little kids, but while working at our medical school, he got into an affair with a graduate student from another department, divorced his wife (I had met her; she was a very nice lady), and married the former graduate student (now a professional person). But the next time I heard about him, he got sick and died at the age of 60. "Sic transit Gloria mundi..." my father used to mind all the time. I was sorry to hear that, after all, he was my colleague... I often thought about him; if he stayed in my department, he would have taken my job as the biochemistry course director when I would have retired (which I did in 2000 A.D. at the age of 65). And then, when my chairman retired in another two years, he may have taken over his chairmanship. He was fairly smart and a native English speaker (not like with a Russian accent); he had all the appropriate properties, but he wanted to reach the top of something sooner than he could have. And he may have avoided getting the cancer disease that killed him.

And so, I am already 86 years old; my former boss and chairman of the Biochemistry Department had died ten years ago, and here I am writing stories about my life's experiences, having buried my beautiful wife in September of the year 2020 A.D., God bless her soul! So why have I chosen to write my Australian colleague's history in the Preface of my book? Perhaps as an excuse to have done less than I could have done in all my life? Perhaps to illustrate the maximum success an immigrant with a Slavic English accent can accomplish in America? My readers have perhaps seen all the TV and radio announcers with British/German accents. But how many have seen speakers with a Slavic accent? I haven't seen one in my 70-year life in America. So perhaps I should shut up and be happy with what I have achieved (especially when I think of my department's chairman with the same education as mine, but with a heavy German accent; the poor fellow died of cancer in his trachea). And I, with the grace of God, have lived already 86 years and yet without any mortal disease threatening, I should not complain about anything; only I still wish that my wife was still alive. She died at the age of 82 of Parkinson's disease, which one of her grandparents brought to the U.S from Belarus! I just hope that my and my wife's sons will not become victims of their great grandmother's Belarus disease but will follow my grandmother, who died when she was 100+ years old and native of Russia's territory on the Caucasian Mountains.

CHAPTER ONE

The Early Years

This book is concerned basically with Marilyn Grib's biography, who became my wife in 1964 and passed away in 2020. If anyone wants to read my life's story, I recommend this author's book titled "All Was Not Lost," Authorhouse Press, Bloomington, IN, 2008, or more recent version, by Author's Tranquility Press, Marietta, GA. Marilyn was 82 years old when she passed away, and I her husband was 85; and I started writing this story a year ago, on March 21, 2021. Marilyn suffered from her illness, Parkinson's Disease, because of her Belorus ancestry, who brought this disease to America. She suffered from this illness for 8+ years, which is a long time; most of its patients pass away 2 to 5 years after diagnosis. Her uncle has lived for four years. And professorial colleague Dr. Gavrilin from Riga University died two years after diagnosis. So the Lord allowed Marilyn to live much longer, thanks to be God for His gift! Marilyn's adopted mother, her uncle's sister from the same family, did not get this awful disease and died in the upper 90's without inheriting it. I hope that my sons will be as successful. Incidentally, neither Marilyn nor I were aware of the fact that her family had Parkinson's' genetics. We found out about that when her uncle came down with it in the 1990s. But I think I still would have married Marilyn!

I met Marilyn at some Russian friend's birthday party in the late 1950s, as I recall when I was still a graduate student and lived with my parents. We dated a couple of times, and somehow, I was able to get a copy of Marilyn's adoption document (fig. 1-1). Marilyn, at the age of 2 ½ months, was adopted and raised by Paula and Nicholas Grib. Her real parents were Paula's brother and wife, members of the same family, who could not support a child (?!). They then left Chicago for California. All that was not a big deal for me; I saw Marilyn whenever I could (or she could since she was attending college). And in 1960, with my Ph. D. degree, I moved to Oak Ridge Tenn, to do post-doctoral work in the Oak Ridge National Laboratory Biology Division. This was a center where the U.S military was building parts for atomic bombs by concentrating uranium element compounds. This required a lot of electricity, and that part of Tennessee had super electricity-creating plants because that area concentrated waterfalls. And all that electricity was required to concentrate the uranium compounds that were necessary to make atomic bombs. And they had a biology division there where they were supposed to invent medications to treat radiation sickness in case of atomic bomb explosions. Thus, the two atomic bombs dropped on Japan in World War II, which ended the war in 1945, were built partly at Oak Ridge. I wasn't hired to work with uranium; my job was at the Biology Division, whose goal was to invent treatment for radiation disease. It was a large Ph. D. scientist employer, but they were never able to invent anti-radiation drugs to treat humans exposed to radiation sickness. And in one year that I spent there, I published some good scientific papers but did not happen to invent a radiation sickness cure and thus earn a Nobel Prize. Marilyn sent me a nice goodbye letter with a "see you later" statement. I did not see her again soon because I did not often go back to Chicago (there were no express-way roads then), but a year later, in 1961, I moved from Oak Ridge to Ames, Iowa, to take another government job in the National Animal Disease Laboratory.

Why Ames? Because there was Iowa State University there with a super veterinary school and the government located their newly-built National Animal Disease Laboratory there. It aimed to invent treatments and/or prevent animal diseases that were frequent invaders of the American farming industry. At that time (in the early 1960's), it employed several dozens of research veterinarians, and it had a biochemistry department with some half-dozen Ph. D. -level biochemists, including me. And it was much easier now to get to Chicago from there. I saw Marilyn quite often after mid-1961. I moved back to Chicago in 1962 after a 2-year stint in the two U. S. government labs, almost like I had been drafted into the military (I did not really get drafted because I had flat feet). In Chicago, I got a professorial job at Rush-Presbyterian-St. Luke's Medical Center, where I stayed teaching medical and graduate students and did research mostly on protein chemistry and iron metabolism for the next 40 years. In that early year of 1962, both my brother and Marilyn were graduating from their colleges, George from the University of Illinois in Urbana with an MS degree in civil/traffic engineering, and Marilyn-with a BA from the National College of Education in Evanston, Illinois. The graduation ceremonies were scheduled at about the same day and time, one in Urbana, Illinois, and the other in Evanston, Illinois. Marilyn got her teacher's degree and a license to teach in elementary schools. I went to George's graduation and expected Marilyn to be mad at me because I did not attend hers. But she wasn't at all angry at me; I was impressed when she said to me that it was more important to go to a brother's graduation than to a girl-friend's one. Or perhaps I was still not "dear" enough for her at that time?

And so, after I returned to Chicago in 1962, after two years away, I began to date Marilyn along with other females that I happened to like. But Marilyn seemed to be an exceptional one, and I always returned to her. In addition, she was of the Orthodox faith who, with her parents, attended the OCA Holy Trinity Russian Orthodox Church, the oldest Orthodox church in Chicago established in 1892 and built in 1902 according to the architect Louis Sullivan's plan based in churches built in Russia's stations of the relatively new Siberian Railroad system that connected Moscow with the Pacific Ocean (fig. 1-2).

Most of the money to build the church was donated by Tsar Nicholas II. Marilyn was baptized there on Dec. 10, 1939 (see fig. 1-3), and, looking at the future, Marilyn and I were married there in 1964.

Speaking of churches, my parents, brother, and I were members of the Holy Virgin Protection Church of Chicago; also Orthodox, where services were conducted in the Slavonic tongue, which is similar to Russian, and our son Gregory, born in 1965, was baptized there. The Holy Virgin Church was founded in 1949 by Russian-speaking, post-World War II immigrants, who did not understand English very much, like my parents. A bit later, Marilyn and I decided to change parishes to Holy Trinity because their services were done in English, which Marilyn understood instead of the Slavonic. I understood both, so it made no difference which language was served in the church I attended. Thus, Alexander, our second son born in 1969, was baptized at the Holy Trinity Cathedral.

After about a year after I returned to Chicago from Ames, Iowa, and after I came to know Marilyn and her family reasonably well, I proposed marriage to her. As a result, I became aware of certain facts about Marilyn's life of which I wasn't aware. She was an adopted child born on June 8, 1938, in Chicago, her parents being one Alex Zickovich (it turned out that he was Paula's brother) and his wife, Violet

Zickovich. Their daughter was named Estelle. For some reason, her parents could not support her, and at the age of 2.5 months, she was given for adoption to Mr. Nicholas Grib and his wife Paula Grib, who renamed the girl Marilyn Jean Grib (see fig. 1-1). The reason why her biological parents could not support her was not indicated, but it seems that they were too poor to support children. Paula's brother and his wife left Chicago shortly thereafter to seek luck in California (and they found it there, as I heard). I do not know if they got divorced there and remarried or remained husband and wife. In the1970's, when Marilyn and I, with our two kids, drove to California for fun and for a Chemistry conference that I had to attend, we met Alex Zickovich (Marilyn's true father) and his wife (we did not know if she was Marilyn's true mother or Alex's second wife), had dinner with them and their two daughters, but our conversations were never related to Marilyn's birth. And unless Alex or his wife would have brought it up, Marilyn nor I did so. We left them as good friends would do but did not leave with any familial information that we didn't know. The next time we saw Alex Zickovich was when John Zickovich, his and Paula's brother (John was a nice man, unmarried, and a lifetime Chicago resident), was deathly ill with Parkinson's Disease and was located at Evanston Hospital. Alex had come to visit his brother before John's expected demise. At that time (in the year 2000), we wanted to have a talk with him, but he refused to meet with us before he returned to California. John Zickovich died shortly after his brother left, and Alex Zickovich must have passed away since then since we heard nothing from him or his family in the last 20 years.

Returning now to little Marilyn after she was adopted by the Gribs, she was baptized in a year+, on December 10, 1939 at the Holy Trinity Cathedral in Chicago with a name of Maria (Mother of God's name), since there is no name of Marilyn in the Orthodox Church registries (see figure 1-3). Marilyn's godfather was Mr. Vasilii (Basil) Sharav (constriction of the Russian Sharavarov), husband of Paula's sister, and the godmother was Olga Tatarchuk (her I had never met). Mr. Sharav was married to Paula's sister and was an engineer by profession, having graduated also from the University of Illinois in Urbana like my brother George did. He was working for the Union Carbide Company in New Jersey. The priest who baptized Marilyn was Father Sergei Snegireff. Marilyn and I were married in the same church on June 14, 1964, by Archbishop John

Garklavs, who formerly was the Bishop of Riga, Latvia, the birth city of mine. For some reason, the Gribs obtained another "Certificate of Birth" for Marilyn dated on 9/22/1954 (she was 15 years old then) (see fig. 1-4), which says her name is Marilyn Jean Grib, that she was born in Chicago on June 8, 1938, from parents Nicholas and Paula (nee Zickovich) Grib, with Nicholas of 41 years of age and Paula of 27. No mention of adoption was mentioned therein, and the fact that the document was phony is indicated that Paula had a hysterectomy at an early age and could have no births whatever. By this document, the Gribs did not want to indicate that Marilyn was adopted. But why so? I never found out.

Marilyn's teens and early twenties were somewhat eventful. Her family lived on the second floor of a 3-storey building at the northern end of Sheridan Road in Chicago, next to the Evanston border. The Gribs were the building's owners (fig. 1-5). The grammar school Marilyn attended was located nearby in Chicago, but for a high school, her parents sent her to a Roman Catholic school for girls in Evanston run by the nuns. I have no idea why they did; perhaps they wanted to have her stay away from boys, but that was not too successful; the student girls were apparently able to find plenty of boyfriends from other schools in town, and Marilyn, after graduation from her high school and at the age of 20, on July 28, 1958, entered into a marriage with a 21-year-old boy from Evanston, without any permission or even knowledge of her parents. Her new husband, Allen F. Eberts, lived in Evanston and was a college student at the Knox College in Galesburg, Illinois. Their marriage was dated on the 26th day of July 1958 on their Marriage License (fig. 1-6). He was obviously at home on his summer vacation when he married Marilyn. I don 't know what occurred after their marriage event, but soon thereafter the bride, through her attorney, started an annulment proceeding via a court in Calumet City, Illinois, which asked the court to cancel the marriage because it was never consummated, and the two of them were together only an hour or two; that the marriage process was the idea of the bridegroom, who wanted to upset his regular girlfriend whom he really loved, and that the marriage with Marilyn was really a phony process by which he wanted to punish his real and true girlfriend. He said that the marriage was not really consummated, and should therefore be annulled (see fig. 1-7). The court believed all that and abolished the marriage without any property exchange or other orders that one usually comes across during regular court divorce proceedings. And so after this adventure, Marilyn apparently entered a teachers college (National College of Education, also in Evanston), and in 4 years got her BA degree and the right to teach elementary school (in 1962). I asked her to marry me in 1963, but she wanted to wait for a year, for 1964. I could not figure out why so long; both of us were getting old and it was time for marriage. I thought that a couple of months to get everything ready was enough. Later on, when I learned about her absolved marriage, it occurred to me that she still hoped that her former Evanston husband would come back to her, but he didn't. So we waited a year; her Ex did not contact her (as far as I know), and we got married on June 8, 1964 at the Holy Trinity Orthodox Cathedral (see chapter 2), and remained so for 56 years, until Marilyn passed away in 2020. On the other hand, there perhaps was no connection with the ghost of Marilyn's former "husband." She just had lots of good time in the early sixties: e. g., often invited to help in weddings (e.g., fig. 1-8 and 1-9), in the 1960's, helping her mother to advertise for Nixon in the 1960 election (fig. 1-10 and 1-11), and during her parents' visits to Florida, participating in weddings there as well (e.g., fig. 1-12). Marilyn was a beautiful young woman and was thus a frequent participant in people's formal events. And perhaps she wanted to participate in these a bit longer when I asked her to marry me, which was OK. By the way, I discovered Marilyn's "ancient" history with her Evanston boyfriend, described above, only after the birth of our son Gregory in 1965. I was very glad that it (the discovery) occurred then and not before our marriage. Otherwise, who knows if we still would have been married if I knew about Marilyn's excessive (?) amorous adventure(s) in the 1950's. Her photo at around our marriage year of 1964 is shown in fig. 1-13, and our marriage ceremony is described in chapter 2 herein.

Fig 1-1

TRANSCRIPT—County Court of Cook County   Form L-208

UNITED STATES OF AMERICA

STATE OF ILLINOIS. \
COUNTY OF COOK \ ss.   *Edward K. Jarecki*

PLEAS before the Honorable THADDEUS V. ADESKO, sole presiding Judge of the County Court of Cook County, in the State of Illinois, at a regular term of said County Court of Cook County, begun and holden at the Court House, in the City of Chicago, in said County and State, in the year of our Lord one thousand nine hundred and...... THIRTY EIGHT ...... and of the Independence of the United States of America the one hundred and.... SIXTY THIRD ......   *Edward K. Jarecki*

Present—THE HONORABLE ~~THADDEUS V. ADESKO~~, \
Judge of the County Court of Cook County.

RICHARD B. OGILVIE, Sheriff of Cook County.

ATTEST: EDWARD J. BARRETT, *Clerk.*

Be it remembered that heretofore, to-wit: on the...... 2ND ......day of...... SEPTEMBER ...... in the year of our Lord one thousand nine hundred and...... THIRTY EIGHT ......, the same being one of the days of the...... SEPTEMBER ......Term of the County Court of Cook County, the following among other proceedings were had and entered of record in said Court, to-wit:

ENTERED

SEP 2 1938

ADOPTION OF CHILD—Decree

STATE OF ILLINOIS, } ss.
COOK COUNTY

IN THE COUNTY COURT OF COOK COUNTY

.....September..... Term, A. D. 1938.

IN THE MATTER OF THE PETITION OF

Nicholas Grib and Paula Grib,

his wife,

TO ADOPT

Estelle Zickovich

92188

ON THIS DAY Come.....the petitioner.s by.......Roy Kroeschell

.....their Attorney, and this cause coming on to be heard upon the petition herein, and evidence adduced by the petitioner.s and the Court having heard the testimony in open Court, and the arguments of counsel, and now being fully advised in the premises, the Court finds that the allegations in said petition are fully proven; that it has jurisdiction of the parties hereto and of the subject matter hereof; That the allegations in said petition are fully proven; that the petitioners herein are husband and wife and reside in Chicago, Illinois, and they desire to adopt Estelle Zickovich, who was born in Chicago, Illinois, on June 8, 1938 to Violet Zickovich and Alex Zickovich, her husband, legal parents.

THE COURT FURTHER FINDS That the parents of said minor child have in writing consented to the adoption of said child by the petitioner.s Nicholas Grib and Paula Grib, his wife,

that said child is a female child, of the age of 21 months year; that its present name is Estelle Zickovich; that the petitioner.s are of sufficient ability to bring up the said child, and furnish suitable nurture and education therefor; and that it is fit and proper that such adoption should be made, and for the best interest of the child.

IT IS THEREFORE ORDERED, Adjudged and decreed, in accordance with the statute in such cases made and provided, that from this date said child Estelle Zickovich shall, to all legal intents and purposes, be the child of the petitioner.s Nicholas and Paula Grib, and for the purposes of inheritance and all other legal incidents and consequences, shall be the same as if it had been born to them in lawful wedlock.

IT IS FURTHER ORDERED, Adjudged and decreed, that the name of said child be changed to Marilyn Jean Grib according to the prayer of the petitioner.s herein.

ON THIS DAY Come......the petitioner.s..by........Roy Krossnell........
..their..Attorney, and this cause coming on to be heard upon the petition herein, and evidence adduced by the petitioner.s..and the Court having heard the testimony in open Court, and the arguments of counsel, and now being fully advised in the premises, the Court finds that the allegations in said petition are fully proven; that..it has jurisdiction of the parties hereto and of the subject matter hereof; that the allegations in said petition are fully proven; that the petitioners herein are husband and wife and reside in Chicago, Illinois, and that desire to adopt Estelle Zickovich, who was born in Chicago, Illinois, on June 5, 1935 to Violet Zickovich and Alex Zickovich, her husband, legal parents.........

THE COURT FURTHER FINDS That the..parents..............of said minor child..have in writing........................consented to the adoption of said child by the petitioner.s..Nicholas Grib and Paula Grib, his wife,.........

that said child is a*..female............child, of the age of..2½ months..........year; that its present name is..Estelle Zickovich........; that the petitioner.s..are.......... of sufficient ability to bring up the said child, and furnish suitable nurture and education therefor; and that it is fit and proper that such adoption should be made, and for the best interest of the child.

IT IS THEREFORE ORDERED, Adjudged and decreed, in accordance with the statute in such cases made and provided, that from this date said child..Estelle Zickovich..........shall, to all legal intents and purposes, be the child of the petitioner.s..Nicholas and Paula Grib and for the purposes of inheritance and all other legal incidents and consequences, shall be the same as if....th.y..had been born to....them..in lawful wedlock.

IT IS FURTHER ORDERED, Adjudged and decreed, that the name of said child be changed to ..Marilyn Jean Grib..............according to the prayer of the petitioner.s..herein.

*Male or Female, as the case may be.

STATE OF ILLINOIS,
COUNTY OF COOK } ss.

JOSEPH J. MC DONOUGH CIRCUIT
I, ~~EDWARD J. BARRETT~~, Clerk of the ~~Superior~~ Court of Cook County, and the keeper of the records and files thereof, in the State aforesaid, do hereby certify the above and foregoing to be a true, perfect and complete copy of ADOPTION DECREE ENTERED: SEPTEMBER 2, 1938 in a certain cause in said Court IN THE MATTER OF THE PETITION OF

NICHOLASS GRIB AND PAULA GRIB

TO ADOPT

ESTELLE ZIOKOVICH

GEN. NO: 92188

In Witness Whereof, I have hereunto set my hand and affixed the Seal of said Court, at Chicago, in said County, this 2ND

No. 72188

COUNTY COURT OF COOK COUNTY

Filed _______ 19___

Clerk.

Attorney.

Certificate of Baptism

Russian Orthodox Greek Catholic Church of
HOLY TRINITY
~~Russian Orth. Greek-Catholic Cathedral~~

1121 N. LEAVITT STREET

This is to certify

That _MARIA GRIB_

Child of _NICHOLAS STEPANOVICH GRIB_

and _PAULINE GRIGORIEVNA (nee ZIHOVICH) GRIB_

born in _CHICAGO, ILLINOIS_

on the _8th_ day of _JUNE_ 19_38_

was

Baptized and Chrismated

on the _10th_ day of _DECEMBER_ 19_39_

According to the Rite of the Russian Orthodox Greek Catholic Church

by the Rev. _SERGIUS SNEGIREFF_

the Sponsors being { _VASILY D. SHAROV_

OLGA CONSTANTINOVNA TATARCHUK

as appears from the ~~Birth~~ Baptismal Register of this Church for 1939.

Dated _May 27, 1964_

HOLY TRINITY CATHEDRAL
1121 N. LEAVITT
CHICAGO 22, ILLINOIS

Emilian Dolansky, Archpriest ________ Pastor

CERTIFIED COPY OF A BIRTH RECORD

254605

CERTIFICATE OF BIRTH

EDWARD J. BARRETT
COUNTY CLERK

Warning: This License is Void if Marriage Ceremony is Not Performed Within 30 Days After Date of Issuance

MARRIAGE LICENSE

To Any Person Legally Authorized to Solemnize Marriage

GREETINGS

Marriage may be Celebrated in the County of Cook and State of Illinois, between Mr. _Allen F. Eberts_ of _Evanston_ in the County of _Cook_ and State of _Illinois_ of the age of __ years and Miss _Marilyn Grib_ at _Chicago_ in the County of _Cook_ and State of _Illinois_ of the age of __ years.

Witness EDWARD J. BARRETT, County Clerk of the County of Cook and the Seal thereof, at my office in Chicago, this __ day of _July_ A.D. 19__

Edward J. Barrett
County Clerk

STATE OF ILLINOIS |
COUNTY OF COOK |

I, _L. William Dickens_, a _Justice of the Peace_, hereby certify that Mr. _Allen F. Eberts_ and Miss _Marilyn J. Grib_ were united in Marriage by me at _City of Evanston_ in the County of Cook and State of Illinois, on the _26th_ day of _July_ 19__

_Wallace _______ Justice of the Peace
Address _1500 Sherman Avenue, Evanston, Ill._

STATE OF ILLINOIS |
County of Cook |

I, EDWARD J. BARRETT, County Clerk of the County of Cook, in the State aforesaid, and Keeper of the Records and Files of said County, do hereby certify that the attached is a true and correct copy of the original Record on file, all of which appears from the records and files in my office.

IN WITNESS WHEREOF, I have hereunto set my hand and affixed the Seal of the County of Cook, at my office in the City of Chicago, in said County.

Edward J. Barrett
County Clerk

STATE OF ILLINOIS)

    | SS

COUNTY OF COOK)

   IN THE CITY OF CALUMET CITY

   OF COOK COUNTY, IN CHANCERY

MARILYN J. EBERTS, Plaintiff)

    Vs. |

ALLEN F. EBERTS, Defendant |

    DECREE FOR ANNULMENT

This cause having come on to be heard upon the Complaint heretofore filed herein,

the Answer of the Defendant , ALLEN F. EBERTS, and the Stipulation of said parties, by their

attorneys, that said cause be heard as in default matters, and the Plaintiff being present in Court

and represented by CHARLES C. COOLEY, ESQ., her attorney , and the Defendant being present

in Court and represented by his attorney , HARRY G. SHULTS, ESQ., and the Court having heard the

testimony being offered and taken in open Court, a certificate of which evidence is filed herein,

and now being fully advised in the premises, DOTH FIND:

1. That it has jurisdiction of the parties hereto and the subject matter hereof.
2. That Plaintiff is a resident of Calumet City, and has been a bona fide resident of the State of Illinois for twenty (20) years last past.
3. That the parties hereto entered into a pretended marriage on or about the 26th day of July, 1958, at Evanston, Illinois.
4. That Plaintiff was fraudulently induced to enter into said pretended marriage in that at the time said pretended marriage took place Defendant had no intention of consummating said marriage in any manner whatsoever, and fraudulently married Plaintiff merely to spite his girlfriend; several hours after the said pretended marriage was entered into said Defendant abandoned and deserted Plaintiff: that Plaintiff has at no time cohabited with said Defendant, and that said marriage was thereby never consummated.
5. That the parties hereto have waived any and all claims each may have or claim to have against the other for alimony, support money, alimony pendente lite , and any and all other claims arising out of said pretended marriage, including homestead rights, dower rights or any other right or rights which either party may have against the other .

ON MOTION of Attorney for the Plaintiff, IT IS THEREFORE ORDERED, ADJUDGED and DECREED and this Court by virtue of the power and authority therein vested, DOTH ORDER, ADJUDGE and DECREE that the pretended marriage entered into between Plaintiff, MARILYN J. Eberts, and the Defendant, ALLEN F. EBERTS, is hereby declared to be null and void and held for naught and said marriage is hereby annulled.

IT IS FURTHER ORDERED, ADJUDGED AND DECREED that the parties heretofore be, and they are hereby barred from any claims each may have or claim against the other for alimony, support money, alimony pendent lite and any and all other claims arising out of said pretended marriage, including Attorneys' fees, Court costs, homestead rights, dower rights, or any other right or rights which either party may have against the other.

Enter ___________________________________
Judge

Dated___________________________

CHAPTER TWO

Marriage of Marilyn and Anatoly and the Aftermath

I asked Marilyn to marry me sometime in the beginning of the 1963 summer. My proposal took place a day after a lengthy date as I brought her home, said good night, and promised to call on the next day. After that, I did a lot of thinking, and on the next day, as I had promised, I called her, and after some chit-chat, I asked her if she would marry me. Yes, on the phone, and not at a fancy meeting on my knees, with a bouquet of flowers and a ring. Instead, it happened during a phone conversation, and surprisingly, she said yes, but she wanted to wait for a year before the wedding ceremony. It sounded like she had already thought about it and had made her decision! Soon thereafter, I bought her an engagement ring with a group of small diamonds that I liked, but she did not like it, and I had to get her another ring with a single 1-carat diamond that she liked. It was twice as expensive as the previous one, but she was worth it, I thought, and indeed she liked wearing it at all times thereafter. Waiting for a year to marry her after my proposal sounded a little peculiar to me; what was there to wait when she was 25 years old, and I was 28, she was well educated (fig. 2-1), had a good job, and I was earning enough to support a family and then some. But most likely, I later thought, she was still waiting for her husband No 1, whom I described in the first chapter herein, to come back to her. But then, in 1963, It sounded peculiar to me since I still did not know about her 1958 marriage to her Evanston boyfriend and its rapid annulment. But he never came back, and I had to lose almost a whole year from staying together with her by waiting for him.

And so, we decided to be husband and wife, and she seemed to be happy with that as I was. There were a number of things that had to be done if everything went as expected: to organize a church wedding, to find an apartment to live in before we could buy a house, to buy furniture, organize a post- wedding festival, and plan post-wedding voyages, Marilyn wanted Archbishop John Garklavs (fig. 2-2) to marry us. I doubted that he would bother with doing this with unimportant people like us, but he did. God bless his soul on Sunday, June 14, 1964. He also signed our marriage license (fig. 2-3). In a way, it may have been so because he was our family's countryman; he was the Bishop of Riga and Latvia until fall 1944 when he and my family left for Germany to escape the Bolshevik rule. And his church was the Riga cathedral, where our family members were parishioners. Archbishop John came to the U. S. in 1949 (after WW II) to join the clergy of the OCA (Orthodox Church of America), which was established in Alaska around the 1780's when that today's U.S. state used to belong to the Russian Empire. America bought that Russian "colony" around 1867, just after the Civil War ended in the U.S. It paid Russia 7.5 million dollars for that wonderful land. If I am not mistaken, Russia used that$ 7.5 million to save the Russian-American Company from bankruptcy and avoid seizure of Alaska by England and its allies following Russia's unsuccessful Crimean War. Our marriage ceremony photos are shown in figs. 2-4 to 2-14.

The festive marriage dinner was organized at Evanston's Orrington Hotel, and in appropriate time, we rented an apartment on Ridge Ave between Touhy and Howard Streets, not far from Marilyn's parents' home on Sheridan Road. I bought the furniture to be delivered before June 14 to make sure it was what Marilyn liked. The apartment was a one-bedroom place on the second floor of the relatively new building, for which I signed a one-year rental agreement. The wedding assistants were invited to arrive early enough, mostly friends of Marilyn. The best man and woman were my brother George and Marilyn's cousin Bonnie Saulnier from New Jersey. The longest job was to write invitations: some 220 persons attended, while 250 were invited. So all that took a bit of time to organize; we could not have had such a fantastic wedding if we were married 3 months after my proposal, and Marilyn was right when she decided on a year of waiting. After the celebration, we went to a nearby hotel. In the morning, I felt that Marilyn would be pregnant in a month as a result, but this did not happen until some 2-3 months later. Greg, our first son, took his time. We left Chicago land very late in the morning and stopped for the night at a motel in Terre Haute, Indiana, and that's where we caught up on our sleep.

We were a happy couple, expecting that our marriage will last forever with the help of everything and everyone, including Archbishop John and the other three priests, who participated with him in our ceremony, who, for sure, also included the good Lord; but it lasted for only 56 years, until November 21, 2020, when Marilyn passed on at the age of 82 because of Parkinson's Disease. But on June 25, 1964, we drove from our Terre Haute Motel with the intention of conquering the world and all diseases existent therein.

Our honeymoon lasted about one month. We visited many towns and cities in Florida, which I don't remember much. I can recall our last stop in Ames, Iowa, on our way back northward, my former habitat, which I wanted to visit before we got back to Chicago. We visited Dr. Roepke in Ames, who was my boss when I worked there, and my landlord with the cat that sometimes didn't let me sleep at night. He always picked up fights at night with other cats right outside my bedroom window (perhaps in a territorial dispute), and many times woke me up at night so that I had to fill a bucket of water and go outside to pour it on the contestants. So the landlord cat did not like me too much. And this time, I found him sleeping in the garage and tried to wake him up to say hello and introduce him to my new wife. But he growled and hissed at me so badly that I was afraid that he might attack Marilyn (I knew how to defend myself against him, and he knew it too), who was standing next to me. So we retreated, and he went back to sleep since he probably again had a rough night. Ames was our last stop on our honeymoon voyage, and the next stop was to Chicago, to our new home. I went to work; Marilyn did too when school started in September of 1964, and soon enough, she became pregnant. Greg decided to get into the world, and he did so in May 8, 1965, about a month before the 1965 summer school vacation began. Greg was a pretty healthy kid, with no problems, weighing over 9 pounds or so, and our obstetrician charged me $225.10 to bring Greg into our world. I asked him what the 10 cents was all about, and he said that he and his nurse had a coffee cup bet (10 cents at that time) about what Greg would weigh. The doctor said 8 pounds, and the nurse said 9+ pounds. The nurse won and had a free coffee cup via my 10 cents. We named our son Gregory, which was the name of Marilyn's grandfather. We had previously decided that Marilyn would name our first son Gregory, and if there was a second one later (there actually was), we would name him Alexander, the name of my grandfather. So, everything was OK, and I was ready to go home with Marilyn and use the baby bed that we had bought and all the other equipment. But Marilyn announced that she was not going home with me but was going to her mother's abode.

She wanted to present her newborn to her mother and not to the child's father, even though she allowed me to visit him once in a while. This was like a blast unto my head from a cannon. I asked her how long she expected to stay with her mother, and she said that she did not know (eventually, it turned out to be 8+ weeks). I asked her if she wanted to leave me, and she said she did not know. This was nothing like what I expected to hear from her. Was it her mother's idea, that is, to leave me? Did she have a boyfriend to whim she would eventually attach herself? But I was allowed to come sometimes to see my son and say hello to him and her. I did that, but I didn't know what to do in the long run. It seemed to me that she wanted to leave me. Why? I absolutely could not figure it out (and I still can't!). When she was going to the hospital to give birth to our son, she was a happy and loving wife, and I was looking forward to having her and our son at home and help her take care of him. And so I started to check my wife's background seriously. As a result (I don't remember how, where, and from whom I got the information about Marilyn's background involving her amorous activities, mainly her marriage to an Allen Eberts in 1958. I described these events in chapter 1 of this book, and unless she organized this run-away effort after Gregory's birth, I would not have known about her previous love affair and first marriage. She was a very pretty young woman (fig. 1-14), and I should not have been surprised about what I found out, but with our serious relationship, she should have told me about it; it is only fair, I think. I am still wondering if there were other affairs of this type, and perhaps even marriages.

However, I had not seriously looked for such others because I was afraid of what I could find (?). So, who knows! But after I learned Marilyn's history with Eberts, I was wondering what to do next. I decided to do nothing for the time being and to see what she would do next. And what happened was that after 8 to 10 weeks after staying with her mother, with Gregory in tow, she came back to me to where I now lived in the apartment that I had prepared for her, the baby, and me together. She came back without saying much, just as if nothing had happened. For me, it was an unexpected surprise! I wonder if it was her mother who forced her to do so, or was it her own decision. But I was happy; I still loved her and, of course, our new son.

At this point, I would like to accelerate our life to 4 years ahead and tell the story of Alex's birth. Alexander was our No. 2 son, born in 1969. Some of the birth events were somewhat different, but I will write about them below. What happened first was that after the birth of son No. 2, I was looking at his birth certificate (still at the hospital), and lo and behold, his name was listed as Nicholas Bezkorovainy, not Alexander Bezkorovainy, as we had agreed to call our No. 2 son. And Nicholas was Marilyn's adopted father's name! I went to the hospital's administration and had son No. 2's name changed to Alexander (Alex). I told Marilyn about that, and she said nothing. When Alex and Marilyn were allowed to go home from the hospital, she again insisted on going to her mother's domicile instead of our home, but her mother said "no cigar." It was now 1969, Greg was four years old, and we already lived in a house in Lincolnwood, Illinois (a suburb of Chicago not far from the Grib home), which we had purchased in 1967 when Greg was 2 years old). It was a stone structure with three bedrooms plus a bathroom on the second floor, and kitchen, dining and living rooms, and a bathroom on the first floor; plenty of space, with a bedroom for each son, and one for Marilyn and me. It was a nice house shown in fig. 2-15, and fig. 2-16 shows Marilyn in the house by the Christmas tree in December 1967. No one could complain that there was not enough living area, like when Greg was born, and we had an apartment with a single bedroom. And so, Paula Grib refused to accept Marilyn with the newborn Alexander in her apartment. Why I don't know, but I was delightful. Perhaps it was Marilyn's punishment because I didn't allow Alex to be named Nicholas? Perhaps now she wasn't sure that Marilyn would go back to me and would want to leave me altogether with the two kids and stay with her (and that she didn't want)? I don't know, but it was a decision that Paula had made, and she stuck with it; a wise decision on her part, regardless of the reason why. That was my thought. That's my opinion! And it avoided a meeting of me with a divorce lawyer, thank be to God. Marilyn, with both kids, was taken by me to our house in Lincolnwood with my enormous joy. Thank you much, Paula! I think you saved our marriage even if you may not have meant to do so. God bless your soul.

After Alex, Marilyn and I had no more children, even though I wanted to have one or two more. Without my knowledge, she started taking anti-pregnancy pills. Quite a bit later, in 2000 A.D., she came down with breast cancer, which is often caused by anti-pregnancy pills, but the Rush doctors saved her life after chemotherapy and surgically removing her cancerous breast (see figs. 2-17 and 2-18). They show Marilyn on a camel by the Egyptian pyramids, which we were visiting, with her hair loss following her chemotherapy. But otherwise, after Alex was born, our life did not have any further difficulties. Marilyn was still visiting Paula almost every day (with kids in tow) before they were both in school, and maybe that was a difficult thing for Paula (?), because the Gribs decided to move to Florida. They had bought a house in Boca Raton that had 3 bedrooms (fig. 2-19), and when the kids were a bit older, we visited them in summers when the kids were on school vacations. Eventually, when the kids got bored with looking at grandparents all day, we bought a condo located on a golf course with 2 bedrooms near Boca Raton for some $40,000, and the kids were playing golf there, often all day, while we visited their grandparents.

During the day, the kids, Marilyn, and the grandparents often went to a beach to do some swimming, and in the evenings, all of us went to a restaurant for dinner. Both the grandparents and the kids enjoyed swimming and sunbathing on the ocean's beaches. The Gribs stayed at Boca Raton until the 1990's when they could no longer manage their lives in Florida on their own (both were over 90 years old). The decision was to bring the Gribs back to Chicago, settle them in a condo on the lakefront, and have Marilyn handle their lives. The condo was bought, and Alex drove to Florida to pick up his grandparents and bring them to their new home in Chicago. But Nicholas got very sick, was taken to the hospital, and died there. He was taken to Chicago for burial, and Paula was also brought to Chicago to live in her condo. She could not live there alone, and we took her to live with us in our townhouse in Lincolnwood. Since in the 1990's we were still working full time, we could not control Paula's life easily, and while we were at work, she would go for a walk all alone, get lost, and the police had to bring her home then. This happened several times, and we finally had to place her in a nursing home, where she stayed safe and sound until she passed on in the late 1990's. Rest in peace, Paula and Nicholas!

We had bought our white stone house in Lincolnwood in 1967 and stayed with it for some 20 years. Greg, by that time, had graduated from college and almost immediately went to live in New York; why New York, I haven't yet figured out. He had $1000 with him, which he asked to borrow from me (he returned it later), but he didn't have a job there yet. It took him a while to get one, as I recall. We advised him to stay at home (free of charge) and find a decent job as long as it would take, but he didn't wish to bother. We had our new house with a large garage and plenty of room, and he could have had a nice room with a place for a car in our large garage (in New York, you have to pay a tremendous rent for a one-car space in a commercial garage). But he wanted to go, and he went. Alex also went to college at Illinois State University in Normal, Illinois, so we no longer had any kids at home, and we thus had space to house other folks that needed housing, relatives, or co-religionists (e. g., Marilyn's uncle when he had his Parkinson's Disease, our friend Victor from Church, who had been kicked out of his house by his wife, who had been looking for a divorce; an Orthodox priest from Ukraine, who came to America to make some money...). We never charged anyone any rental money, and it was sometimes fun because our kids were no longer with us, and we had someone to talk to in the evening.

When both of our kids were spending their almost entire days in school, Marilyn went back to work as a teacher. In the evening, when I was at home with the kids, she took some classes at Northeastern Illinois University, basically a teachers' college, to get an MA degree in Special Education. She got her degree in 1981(fig. 2-20 and 2-21). Her first job was with the Tikvah Institute run by a Carolyn Brenner, who started this organization in 1967. It had only ten students, and it was Hebrew-oriented. Its supporters were Jewish doctors and other moneyed professionals. Unfortunately, Ms. Brenner got into some kind of disagreement with her supporters, their money ceased to come, and Marilyn lost her job. She was terribly upset with losing her first job, but I think I could calm her down by convincing her that nothing happened because of her fault and that the issues were due to the school's financial supporters. And Marilyn was soon invited to join a Roman Catholic school, called Little Sisters' School for Retarded Children, which functioned to help mentally disabled children, run by nuns whose head was Sister Maria Bernadette (fig. 2-22). They accepted children who could not be handled by the Chicago public schools, and thus their money came not from the student families but from the Chicago Board of Education. Still, compared to the teachers' salaries of the Chicago Board of Education, Marilyn's salary was only one-third of theirs. Still, she liked her colleagues, the nuns and fellow teachers and remained with them for ten years. She left because the principal priest that had hired her had died, and his replacement had destroyed the school's teaching structure; the school was closed as a result.

Because Marilyn had all the diplomas for teaching special children and was a popular teacher, the school's leaders and colleagues had called her "principal" (fig. 2-23). Sister Bernadette was really the principal, but she did not mind; she too liked Marilyn a lot. The kids were usually sent to her school by Chicago's special education teachers who could not handle their "patients." The teachers in the Catholic school were more successful with the retarded kids than the public schools were; they had to handle fewer kids per teacher, and perhaps they were "nicer" and more patient toward them. The parents understood this, they were very supportive of the Catholic school, and there were many "waiting" students/patients whose parents wanted the private school to teach their kids as opposed to public schools. But the good times did not last forever; the pastor of the church, who was also the school's principal, died, and a new priest was appointed to run the place. This was not the normal Catholic church under the Roman pope but a "Catholic Church" established in Italy in the 19th century by some priests who were unhappy with the pope. They claimed that they wanted to become Orthodox, yet they did nothing to accomplish this for 100 years, so why didn't they, I would ask them? No answer! They had plenty of time since the start of the 19th century. But of course, they did not change anything from the Catholic to the Orthodox faiths; they simply did not like the pope and his organization to be their master, and that was all. But they never bothered Marilyn to change her religion from the Orthodox faith to theirs, and in general, they were very nice to her, and she liked working there even if her pay was minimal.

The new boss was appointed by the church's leadership, whoever they were, but definitely not connected with the pope of Rome. And the new boss was a totally different person; he didn't like women, and especially the nun Bernadette, Marilyn's real boss and financier of the school (a good one). She was the person who maintained the school in the "black" financial condition (as opposed to the "red"), and treated the teachers like colleagues quite well. Not the new chief priest and boss; I forget all the issues that the "new" chief created, only that several of the school workers were fired or sued in courts for all kinds of "crimes," such as Marilyn's defense of her fellow teachers of crimes invented by the new leader (I don't know why he simply didn't fire them; I think that he wanted to somehow win money from them by accusing them of "damages" that they somehow developed). Marilyn defended her colleagues, and her new boss took her to court as well. There, I don't remember what she was being accused of by her boss. Marilyn was defended by a lawyer appointed by the State Farm Insurance Co., to whom we were paying an annual (and relatively cheap) premium against personal suits. Marilyn's suit, defended by a good lawyer (paid by State Farm), was dismissed immediately. The other folks who did not have such insurance had to go to trial, most of which (if not all) were also dismissed. But it took time and money. Marilyn and her colleagues were, of course, "fired" from the school, and the new Fuehrer (leader) took over the school, which immediately collapsed. I don't know what happened to the parish; they may have moved elsewhere, but its old building has been converted into a condo. Sister Bernadette opened a new school (not associated with any churches), and did a reasonably good job (I am told) with the kids. She hired Marilyn, on a part-time basis, to be like an advisor for her teachers because Marilyn had all the credentials and experience. Sister Bernadette wanted Marilyn to work for her again on a full-time basis, but Marilyn was already working full-time in Chicago's Public School System as a special education teacher earning a salary three times higher than she had earned with Sister Bernadette. In addition, she had all the union benefits given by the Chicago Teachers' Union. She remained with the Chicago teachers' group for 15 years retiring at the age of 62 in the year if 2000.

The year 2000 was also my semi-retirement year; that's when I turned 65 years old and switched my job from the full-timer to part-timer. But in addition, I took a part-time job with another Chicago medical school to teach biochemistry to their first-year students. I kept these two jobs for another five years until the age of 70 (the year 2005), when I retired "lock, stock, and barrel" and moved with my wife to live in Galena, Illinois. We already had a small house in Galena; as I recall, we bought it in A. D. 2000, and we used to go there on weekends and stay there longer if we had no classes in Chicago schools where we still taught. And so in 2005, we sold our cottage and bought a larger house on a ½ acre lot, where we stayed for the next ten years. Initially, we thought we would stay in Galena forever, but it didn't happen: in 2010, the doctors discovered Parkinson's Disease in Marilyn's system; we were also told that the Galena/Dubuque doctors could not take care of it, so we have to move somewhere else, where such specialists are. After thinking of all probabilities, we decided to move to where Alex lives, i. e., Phoenix, Arizona. One reason was that there was a special clinic financed by a boxing champion (Mohamed Ali) who had this disease, and they could then take care of Marilyn. We decided to move there, but we couldn't sell our house in Galena until 2015.

Meanwhile, we bought a smaller house in Sun Lakes, Arizona, where we stayed in wintery times with Marilyn being treated by specialists, and the rest of the year, we stayed back in Galena. Finally, in 2015, we sold our Galena house for $180,000 (we bought it for $260,000 in 2005) and moved to Arizona "lock, stock, and barrel." Marilyn was already quite weak but was still walking and otherwise functioning, and now things got a bit easier when we did not have to travel some 1500 miles twice a year. Figure 2-24 shows the Bezkorovainy family at a Chandler restaurant in 2015. Standing left to right are Anatoly Bezkorovainy and his wife Marilyn; sitting are Gregory Bezkorovainy with his wife and two daughters; standing are Alexander Bezkorovainy and Deacon Alexis Washington (of blessed memory) of our Sts. Peter and Paul Church. Marilyn, of course, passed away at the end of the 2020's year, and I am still alive in the mid-2021 st year, visiting Marilyn's grave with our son Alex twice a week; God bless her soul!

NATIONAL·COLLEGE·OF·EDUCATION

EVANSTON·ILLINOIS

ON THE RECOMMENDATION OF THE FACULTY AND BY
VIRTUE OF THE AUTHORITY VESTED IN THEM THE
TRUSTEES OF THE COLLEGE HAVE CONFERRED ON

MARILYN JEANNE GRIB

THE DEGREE OF

BACHELOR OF EDUCATION

GIVEN IN THE CITY OF EVANSTON ILLINOIS IN THE
YEAR OF OUR LORD ONE THOUSAND NINE HUNDRED
SIXTY-TWO ON THE ELEVENTH DAY OF JUNE

Christian E. Jarchow
President of the Board of Trustees

K. Richard Johnson
President

JUL 22 1964
EDWARD J. BARRETT
COUNTY CLERK
FORM 44
STATE OF ILLINOIS } s.s
COUNTY OF COOK
Marriage License
NO. 2747160
RETURNED AND
FILED DATE JUN 1 9 1964
To Any Person Legally Authorized to Solemnize Marriage
Greetings
Marriage may be celebrated in the County of Cook and State of Illinois,
between Mr ANATOLY BEZKOROVAINY of Chicago, in the County of Cook
and State of Illinois, of the age of 29 years, and MISS MARILYN JEAN GRIB
of Chicago, in the County of Cook and State of Illinois, of the age of 26 years.
Witness Edward J. Barrett, County Clerk
of the County of Cook, and the Seal thereof,
at my office in Chicago, this 8 day of
JUNE A.D. 1964
Edward J. Barrett
County Clerk
The person who solemnizes this Marriage, and all other persons, are cautioned against
making any changes in this License.
State of Illinois } s.s. I, ARCHBISHOP JOHN an ARCHBISHOP
County of Cook
Name of person officiating   Official Title
hereby certify that Mr ANATOLY BEZKOROVAINY and MISS MARILYN JEAN GRIB
were united in Marriage by me at CHICAGO in the County of Cook, and
State of Illinois, on the 14 day of JUNE 1964.
Signature and official title
THE NAMES IN THIS CERTIFICATE MUST BE
IDENTICAL WITH NAME ON ABOVE LICENSE.
Address
N.B. THIS LICENSE WITH CERTIFICATE OF MARRIAGE PROPERLY MADE OUT MUST (WITHIN 30 DAYS) BE RETURNED TO THE COUNTY CLERK BY THE PERSON WHO PERFORMED THE WEDDING CEREMONY
STATE OF ILLINOIS,
County of Cook.
I, EDWARD J. BARRETT, County Clerk of the County of Cook, in the State aforesaid,
and Keeper of the Records and Files of said County, do hereby certify that the attached is a
true and correct copy of the original Record on file, all of which appears from the records and
files in my office.
IN WITNESS WHEREOF, I have hereunto set my hand and
affixed the Seal of the County of Cook, at my office in the City of Chicago,
in said County.
Edward J. Barrett
County Clerk

UPON THE RECOMMENDATION OF THE FACULTY
AND BY AUTHORITY OF THE BOARD OF GOVERNORS OF
STATE COLLEGES AND UNIVERSITIES

NORTHEASTERN ILLINOIS UNIVERSITY

HAS CONFERRED UPON

MARILYN GRIB BEZKOROVAINY

THE DEGREE OF

MASTER OF ARTS

WITH ALL OF THE RIGHTS, HONORS AND PRIVILEGES BELONGING TO
THAT DEGREE. IN WITNESS THEREOF THIS DIPLOMA IS GRANTED
THIS MONTH OF APRIL, 1981.

CHAPTER THREE

Marilyn's Married Life

This is the last chapter of Marilyn's life story; she was an unusual personality among 320+ million Americans that managed to overcome numerous life's obstacles and brought joy and happiness to many individuals including the authors of this booklet. She decided to quit work at the age of 62 after about 15 years working in Chicago's public school system teaching mentally challenged students. Before that, she worked in private schools that were handling retarded kids and whose parents were helpful and cooperative with teachers, and the results were successful insofar as the kids learned how to study and reading books. In public schools, most parents were not helpful; when teachers had contact with parents and asked them for help at home, they were told " you are teacher, you help him/her..." The parents were not impressed when they were told that "retarded" kids must be taught 24/7, not just an hour or two in school, where a teacher has perhaps a dozen kids and needs to help them all. And Marilyn, at the age of 62, could no longer take it one day, she came home crying; a kid attacked her, and when she attempted to defend herself, another teacher observed the situation and stepped in (thanks be to God for that). Both the kid and Marilyn were quieted down. When Marilyn came home, she told me that she quit work; she should not have lost her temper. I said, "let us do it in an orderly fashion. It was winter time, and let us wait until the academic year is over in June, and you can then retire if you want." And that is what she said did. In June 2000, the school organized a big party for Marilyn with all the teachers and administrators attending. Marilyn was allowed to invite guests, including me and many of our friends at our church, including our Orthodox priest, Father Sergey Garklavs, with his wife. Even the nun, Sister Bernadette, who was the principal at the Catholic Church school where Marilyn worked for some 10 years, but had to close it. Her former boss, Sister Bernadette, organized a new school and invited Marilyn to be its principal, but Marilyn had already accepted the job in the Chicago Board of Education and did not want to upset them. This all happened in 1985, and as far as we know, Sister Bernadette ran her new school successfully until she retired into a convent some 25+years later. And Marilyn was now retiring at the age 62 after being a Chicago teacher for 15 years. The Chicago retirees got nice pension money (dependent on years worked) and Blue Cross medical insurance (hurray to the union membership). Photograph 3-1 indicates Marilyn's work last year in the Little Sisters School run by Sister Bernadette with Marilyn as the principal teacher, and 3-2 indicates the way we looked when Marilyn came to work for the Chicago teacher' system (1985).

To celebrate Marilyn's retirement from the Chicago school system, its administration and faculty organized a grand party in June 2000 A.D We were permitted to invite as many persons as we wanted to the farewell party. There were probably nearly as many guests as at our wedding. The party took place on a Saturday in a restaurant in Berwyn, Illinois, on 22nd Street, with Father Sergey Garklavs saying the prayers and speeches by Marilyn's school principal and her colleagues. Among our friends that came to our meeting, many are no longer with us: Father Sergey Garklavs and his wife (figs. 3-4 and 3-6), Dr. Leo

Topouzian (fig. 3-5), and Mr. and Mrs. George Pradun (fig. 3-9). God bless their souls!

And so, by June 2000 A.D., my wife became retired, and I became partly retired. My retirement was not particularly celebrated. Certainly not like Marilyn's who was at the Chicago school for 15 years, whereas I was at Rush for 40+ years. One little celebration was my appointment to lead our graduating medical students to the stage to get their M.D. diplomas. Figure 3-12 shows my persona clothed in the Ph. D. robe and carrying a bag, Leading the Rush Medical College 2000 A. D. graduating class to receive their diplomas. There were no festive retirements parties for me other retiring professors, which was just fine by me. Actually, I retired only part-time and acquired another part-time job at the Chicago Medical School located in a northern Chicago suburb. At Rush, I was teaching a part of a medical student biochemistry course. Both of us now had some free time, and we used the weekends to visit the historical town of Galena in northern Illinois by the Mississippi River. We liked Galena so much that we bought a small house there (fig. 3-13), between $150,000-160,000 dollars' worth, and visited it almost every weekend. A convenient thing was the presence of a Greek Orthodox church in the city of Dubuque, Iowa, across the Mississippi River, that we could attend on Sundays. The house was a 900 sq. foot 2-storey cottage with 2 bedrooms and 2 baths. One bedroom and bath were on the first floor, the second was on the second floor; pretty convenient for visitors who were placed on the first floor, and we remained on the second one. And we now had frequent visitors on the weekends, e.g., Victor Owczaruk (fig. 3-14), or Berverly Dubin(fig. 3-15), who both liked to visit the farm animals near our house. Figure 3-16 shows us, a happy couple, in the kitchen of our little house.

One evening in 2005, on the weekend, Marilyn and I were walking on the pretty crowded Main Street of Galena, And all of a sudden, there came a suggestion into my head that we should move to Galena "lock, stock, and barrel." I asked what Marilyn thought about that, and she said, "let's do it." And we did! We sold our small 900 square foot cottage (fig. 3-13) and bought a bigger house in the same area as the cottage we had, $260,000 with 3 large bedrooms, 2 1/2 car garage, 3 1/2 baths, and a half-an-acre lot (fig. 3-17). Then I quit my two part-time jobs in Chicago, and we moved to Galena "lock, stock, and barrel," and didn't even look back into Chicago as we left it. We loved living there, but 10 years later, in 2015, we had to move to Arizona where Alex lived because Marilyn was hit by Parkinson's Disease was not so rare where we were in Chicago. I met its patients much more often. But we'll talk more about Parkinson's Disease below, and now, we will talk about our life in Galena.

We spent about 10 years in Galena, from 2005 to 2015, though around 2010 we decided to spend our winters in Arizona. This was the time when Marilyn began to feel her Parkinson's Disease more seriously every year, and winter-time was difficult for her to tolerate in Galena. The last time we went to Europe was in 2007, when we again visited Russia and another group of European countries. After the trip, which lasted some 4 weeks, we no longer traveled outside the U.S.; at least our passports don't indicate travels beyond 2007 to Russia and neighboring countries. It was a wonderful trip, but Marilyn had difficulties getting in or out of busses, was tired easily, and falling down often. One fall was in Vilnus, Lithuania, where she was getting into a bus at our hotel. She was taken to an "American Hospital," where X-rays were taken, but they showed that nothing was broken, thank God, only bruises occurred, this was in 2007, and beyond that trip, we never went beyond the USA borders. Yet that last trip was quite interesting: we flew into Russia in St. Petersburg, where we visited my relatives, the Dobriakovs and other interesting places, and got on a river passenger boat (very comfortable and well managed), which, via rivers and canals, including the Volga River, took us into Moscow with numerous stops to visit and investigate Russian cities and countryside. The ship took us to Moscow, where we spent several days visiting various places, including my cousin, the doctor (today, blessed memory), the Kremlin with its museums, and the Christ the Savior Cathedral (fig. 3-18), which can be visited a dozen times and still not light the candles at all the icons. After several days in Moscow, we got in a bus and drove westward on a pretty solid and rapid highway into Minsk, Belarus, where we stopped in a hotel overnight. Belarus is now an independent country (in the Tsarist and Soviet eras, it was a part of Russia), so we had to get visas that were glued into our passports on a page next to the Russian visas (3-19 and 3-20). The bus, on the next day, took us to the Lithuanian border (we weren't taken for any sightseeing rides in Belarus; perhaps there are no interesting tourist attractions in that country?), where we got stuck for some time. It was no fault of the Russians or Lithuanians; the Belarus border guards were asking our Russian driver for something; everyone's passports were checked and were passed, yet something else was missing. Finally, our driver walked back into the bus, opened a small closet next to his seat, and pulled out a 2-liter bottle of Smirnoff vodka, He took it to the guard house, and in 5 minutes, the bus had crossed the Belarus-Lithuanian border. The Lithuanians did not even stop us, and let us drive through directly into Vilnus, the Lithuanian capital. We stayed there for several days; it is a beautiful city. Of interest is the main street, whose name I do not remember. It was straight as an arrow. We were told by our guide that such geometry was ordered by the Russian military governor after Russian had won its Napoleonic war of 1812, and part of Poland and all of Lithuania were joined to Russia (today, Lithuania is an independent nation). The governor noted that the city's main street was geometrically uneven with many turns, ends, and restarts, and he ordered to rebuild the street into an arrow-like appearance with new stores, hotels, and theatres, i.e., to look like a true main street of a new Russian provincial capital. Driving northward with our bus, we, with a few stops, crossed the Latvian border, visited the city of Jelgava (Mitau in German). The Duchy of Mitau even had colonies on the American continent. We visited the palace of the duke, which is now a museum. Today and in the first era of Lavian independence (1918-1940), Latvia was divided into 4 provinces: Kurzeme (Liepaja capitol), Zemgale (Jelgava/Mitau capitol), Vidzeme (Riga capitol), and Latgale (Rezekne capitol). During the Tsarist Russian era (1710-1918), Latvia had 2 Russian gubernias (provinces): Kurland with Jelgava/Mitau as capitol and Livland with Riga as capitol. And so, after visiting the city of Jelgava, an interesting city where I had never been before when I lived in Riga (1935-1944), we went to Riga, my birth place, now the capitol of Latvia (population 2.5 million in all Latvia). We stayed there several days, where we visited our former living quarters on Stabuiela (Street), and before that, on Reval Street. The Orthodox Cathedral, where I was baptized in 1935, was closed by the Bolsheviks and converted into an astronomical observatory. But now, it is an Orthodox cathedral again in all its glory. The city of Riga today looked exactly like what I remember as a kid; nothing changed; all the new buildings built during the Soviet era in Riga were the city's suburbs, which had nothing to admire. After Riga, we drove to Tallin, Estonia, and after a few days there, we took a boat across the Bay of Finland to Helsinki, where we took the plane back to Chicago. This was our last trip to foreign lands because Marilyn did not feel well most of the time on the trip, and we stayed home or drove to neighboring interest communities by car in order to investigate our relatively new living "country." And there were plenty such places, events, or happenings to keep one busy.

Galena is a beautiful little city, older than Chicago, and its name originated because there was lead mining activity in the area ("galena" is the chemical name of lead ore), and as a result, there were manufacturing of lead bullets in the city and neighboring towns during the U.S Civil War. But now, there is no lead mining or bullet manufacturing in the area, and Galena is a commercial and tourist/visitors' center today. There are numerous early and late 19th century structures in town, and as an example, we are showing the three of them hereby: figs 3-21, 3-22, and 3-23. They are, respectively, Galena city with Grant Park's statues of the General; the "Belvedere House," today a hotel; and General/Present's Grant house with Marilyn, my wife, standing in front of it. The latter was built by the Galena city people for General Grant and his family to live in after the Civil War, but the General lived there only a few months as he was elected the U.S president and lived in

Washington D.C. with his family. After two presidential terms, he lived in New York and died there, never returning to Illinois. His house in Galena is now a museum. Galena was our home for some 15 years 2000-2015, and I can say that for me, it was the most pleasant place in my life. To make some things clearer, I would like to construct a list of our developments in Galena from the beginning to end, even though Marilyn was sick in the last few years of our Galena Residence.

Year	Event(s)
	Marilyn retired as a teacher; I retired from full-time work at Rush Medical College.
2000	We bought a small house on the Galena Territory and spent most of our weekends there.
2005	I retired totally from Rush Medical College and Chicago Medical School.
2005	We sold our houses in Galena and Lincolnwood and bought a bigger one on Galena.
2007	We went on a trip to Russia and neighboring countries.
2010	Marilyn was diagnosed with Parkinson's Disease.
2011	My aunt Vera Kijauskas passed away at the age of 99; buried at Greenwood Cemetery. We put our Galena house for sale and bought a house in Sun Lakes, Arizona.
2014	We celebrated 50 years of our marriage.
2015	We sold our house in Galena Territory and moved to Sun Lakes, Arizona.
2020	Marilyn passed away on Nov. 21 at age of 82 & was buried on Nov. 30, 2020 at Greenwood Cemetery in Phoenix, Arizona. My place will be next to Marilyn's when the time comes.

And so, after our last trip to Russia and other East European countries in 2007, we settled down in Galena, enjoying its frequent events, and traveling to nearby communities or other U.S. areas (like Arizona) once in a while. Just in our area, there were always some events being organized that attracted tourists and all you had to do to participate was to exit your hotel room (if you were a "local," your nearby home) and join the parade as a participant or observer. Unlike big cities, where attending such events in a city's downtown costs a fortune to park your car, and the thousands of viewers can crush you to death! In Galena, such events were great fun, and you could participate therewith: see figures 3-24 to 3-26 (a parade on Galena's Main Street), figures 3-27 and 3-28 (Marilyn's balloon ride), and the kids at an auto show (fig. 3-29). Marilyn and I also celebrated the July 4 Independence Day: as shown in pictures 3-30, both of us were dressed up and had a U. S. flag flying over our house door. Next to picture 3-30 is 3-31, which shows a waterfall that starts a small river that picks up excess water from the Galena Lake and sends it down to the Mississippi River. When it rains, the waterfall delivers lots of water to the Mississippi River, but if it doesn't rain for a week or so, the waterfall practically ceases to exist.

As I stated above, Marilyn and I did not seriously travel beyond the U.S. On the other hand, we had plenty of visitors that paid visitations to us in the years of 2007 to 2015. And we too traveled to the U. S. to visit our relatives or friends. For instance, Dr. Aydelotte from the Biochemistry Department at Rush visited us in 2006 when she and her husband visited their relatives in Lena, Illinois, a few miles east of Galena, Illinois (fig. 3-32). Beverley Dubin visited us many times, including the animals in a neighboring farm (fig. 3-33, taken on 3/1/07).

Beverley Dubin's husband, Alvin Dubin, was Anatoly's colleague as a professor at the University of Illinois, though his main job was chief of the Cook County Hospital's biochemistry laboratories. He was a good friend of ours (he was born in Russia but came to the U.S. as a child), yet still could speak Russian. He died fairly early, in his 70's; God bless his soul. Then there was my aunt and godmother, Vera Kijauskas, who was born in 1912 and lived in Phoenix, Arizona; her husband had passed away a long time ago. Her married daughter Nora is also a widow with the last name of Frost; she lives in Scottsdale. My brother and I used to play with her on our grandfather's farm in Lithuania in the summers of 1942-1944. We saw Vera and Nora often after we moved to Sun Lakes, but perhaps not often enough. Marilyn and I missed Vera's death and funeral in 2011, and I don't recall why! Photo 3-34 shows Vera on her 96th birthday, photo 3-35 shows Vera and Anatoly with Vera's Christmas tree in 2006, and 3-36 shows Ella, Gregory, Alex, Nora, Aunt Vera, and Marilyn at Christmas time in the year of 2006--2007. I was probably the photographer. The closest "big" city to Galena, Illinois, was Dubuque, Iowa. It has about 150,000 inhabitants and is located on the Mississippi River. If one can't get something in Galena, one goes to Dubuque. It has two superb hospitals with good physicians and excellent surgeons. Both I and Marilyn had surgeries done, and they came out perfectly. Perhaps this is because they do not have residencies and, therefore young and inexperienced resident surgeons. Both of us had surgeries done there, and they were superbly done; better than at Presbyterian-St. Luke's Hospital. But they could not treat Parkinson's Disease. One of their super neurologists diagnosed it in Marilyn: he told her to walk the length of a room, turn around twice, then walk back. She did it all, except that she turned around only once. And the neurologist said she had Parkinson's Disease. And unfortunately, they could not treat it; she had to go to the University of Illinois Rockford Medical School or to Iowa City's University of Iowa Medical school. Both are over 100 miles from Galena. Or else, we had to return to Chicago, which we didn't want to do. This diagnosis was performed in the year of 2010, but we could not sell our house in Galena until 2015 (i.e., 5 years later); there was a recession, which led to house costs dropping tremendously, and in "Galena Territory," where our house was located, every other house was for sale. We had to drop the price of our house from $260,000 (that's what we paid for it) to $180,000 (that's what we sold it for), and still had no offers for 5 years! In the winter of 2010-2011, we went to where Alex lived in the Phoenix area, and until we sold our house in the Galena Territory, we used to spend our winters there. The temperatures in Phoenix were much warmer, no snow in winter, and Marilyn was much more comfortable there. We also contacted a Parkinson's Disease specialist doctor whom we saw every month when we were there (Nov. 10 to about April 15) and much more often when we moved there permanently in 2015. And finally, we bought a house in Sun Lakes, a suburb of Phoenix, for a price of $175,000 in the year of 2010, which has 3 bedrooms, 2 baths, and a two-car garage with a living area of 1900 sq. feet. It was somewhat smaller than our Galena house, but that was OK! Alex was telling us to rent it out when we were in Galena, but we didn't do it, and I think that it was a good decision. It remained in good shape, and I am still living there (fig. 3-37). We paid off its cost when we sold our Galena house in 2015. That's when we moved to Arizona "lock, stock, and barrel" (again), and we haven't been in Galena since then. But between the years of 2010 and 2015, we explored Northwestern Illinois and Southern Wisconsin more thoroughly, and the next paragraph describes those years.

Let us start with Dubuque, Iowa. It is an interesting city on the Western part of the Mississippi River. It has 100,000 to 150,000 inhabitants and 2 super hospitals (but no Parkinson's Disease specialists). There is a Greek Orthodox Church which we attended while we lived in Galena for the first couple of years and then moved further East to a Russian church. The reason was its rich members, the Archons: one who owned half of the stores in Dubuque and another who was the owner of a factory, i. e., the moneyed men. They controlled which priest was hired and which was retained. My wife and I became friendly with both priests who were there when we were, and in our opinion, both were spiritually superb, yet disagreed about some things with the two Archons: One of them even took me to dinner and asked what I thought about the spirituality of one of them as if I was an expert on such matters. And I demurred to answer what he expected. I liked and respected both of the priests and could not criticize them. Nevertheless, both were fired within 2 years. As a result, Marilyn and I left as well, and we joined a Russian Orthodox Church near Rockford, Illinois, the trip to which on Sunday mornings took about an hour and 15 minutes instead of the 10 minutes it took to get to the Dubuque church from Galena. I still correspond with one of the Greek priests who is now retired; may God bless him! Fig. 3- 38 shows Marilyn and a Greek parishioner selling Lenten food at the Greek Church before a feast day, and fig. 3-39 shows the Greek ladies with Marilyn celebrating the Greek priest's birthday in September 2007. But we changed our membership to the Rockford Russian church until we moved to Arizona; after all, they have no Archons. While we were there for several years, nothing happened to the Russian priest, a retired engineer with a job at a Rockford factory and was quite friendly with his bishop, who often came from Chicago to serve at the Russian community.

We took several of our guests to Dubuque to show them that nice city. Photo 3-40 and 3-41 shows the visit of our Chicago priest Father Sergey Garklavs, adopted son of Bishop John of Riga and Chicago. Photo 3-40 is showing a bridge, the only one across the Mississippi River in Dubuque. On the West side of the river is the State of Iowa, and on the East side is Illinois. So, Dubuque is in Iowa, and Galena is in Illinois. With Father Sergey is his wife with a blue blouse, Marilyn with a green blouse, and Beverley Dubin is on the right side of the group. They are in Iowa. I was taking the photo. Another similar one is 3-113 (p.148) at the Mississippi River harbor with Father Sergey, his wife, Marilyn, and me, with Beverley Dubin as the photographer. At the back of me is a river boat, "Spirit of Dubuque," on which we took a ride, also shown on the postcard 3-41. Some other Dubuque pictures are 3-42, the city tower clock; 3-43, the Dubuque court house; 3-44, the Dubuque history story, and 3-45, the Dubuque "elevator" that takes tourists on a town's hill that avoids one to climb up there on stairs. On that hill, you can see pretty much the entire city of Dubuque located on the shore of the Mississippi River and the rail "busses" that take tourists down the hill rather rapidly.

Another immigration-important city in our area was New Glarus, established by Swiss immigrants to the U.S. in the late 1700's. Their grandfather is considered to be Fridolin Legler {1791-1868) (fig. 3-46}. He is buried in the Swiss immigrant cemetery in New Glarus, Wisconsin (fig. 3-47 and 3-48). This was a group of Swiss immigrants who were looking for religious freedom and had acquired some Protestant faith that their government did not approve of. So like many others, they came to the U. S. and settled in Wisconsin. Their town is between Madison, Wisconsin, and the northern border of the State of Illinois. Their church is similar to typical Protestant churches and is also located in New Glarus (fig. 3- 49). New Glarus is full of various stores, which are impossible to oversee in a day or two. There are also many statues of cows and other animals (fig. 3-50) and Swiss-style buildings (fig. 3-51). Marilyn and I have been there several times and always found something new. A couple of other peculiar buildings that one can see on the roads of Illinois, Wisconsin, and Iowa are in Nora, Illinois, whose building methodology is absurd. It is shown in fig. 3-52. I don't know why it was built that way, but now it is a storage place. Then there is a building on cross-roads (I forget which village it is) that used to be a store with the store owner living on the second floor (fig. 3-53). One day, the wind was a bit rough, and the building tilted like it looks today. Its owners ran away, but the building did not collapse, and for years, it is now sitting there like that at a rural road intersection. Then, near the Illinois border, there is a village called New Diggings, which used to house miners of a nearby mine (I believe that it was some metal ore mine). It has a monument of the World War I times, which listed its high school graduate class of 1917, who went into the U. S. World War I army in their entirety. All their names are listed on the monument. They did not list any members of the graduate class who were killed in the war. Maybe there weren't any, we hope, but there was a total of 30 names. Some 100 years ago, there apparently was a town here that had a high school. Today, there are only 2 public buildings: a general store (fig. 3- 54} and a tavern. One can also see two farm houses nearby. Photo 3-55 shows Marilyn in a State Park in Florida, probably around 2010, but that's a different story.

One of the more important happenings in 2014 was the celebration of Marilyn's and Tony's son, wedding anniversary on June 14, 2014. It was done in an Oak Park hotel where we had some 200 guests like we had at our wedding. Marilyn's cousin Bonnie Saulnier was there with us, but she too was not looking very healthy. We later found out that she had a cancerous disease, which killed her soon thereafter (God bless her soul). But there were other guests whom we loved to see, like the entire family of George's daughter, including the colonel, her husband, as well as the kids. And even Tatiana's brother Alex, the diving expert, was there. Father John Adamcio chaired the guest meeting by serving a short molieben, and thanks to him, we were able to thank the Lord for our successful 50 years together and ask for another stretch of "happy days," if possible, which the Lord did extend for another 6 years.

Marilyn, my brother George, Cousin Nora Frost, and I are shown in pictures No. 3-56. Next year, in the year of 2015, we managed to sell our house in Galena Territory and moved to Sun Lakes, Arizona, near where Alex, our son, has his house in the city of Chandler. Before our move, we had purchased a house there (fig. 3-37), and moved there "lock, stock, and barrel" in the Summer of 201S. After we settled down in our new living quarters, we decided to confirm what disease Marilyn had acquired some years ago, and her doctor (Dr. Ku), whom we saw upon arrival in Sun Lakes, sent her to a hospital that specialized in such diseases that we suspected had settled in Marilyn. She stayed there for 10 days, and the diagnosis was the same as what we suspected: Parkinson's Disease. And Dr. Ku then transferred Marilyn to a specialist on this disease in a Phoenix Hospital, which, for the next 3 years, was where Marilyn was visiting him every month practically. She could no longer walk and had to be moved in a wheel chair. The experts charged some $400-$600 per visit but did not improve anything, and Marilyn had become bed-ridden, eventually, we could no longer take her to the hospital to visit doctors. We had to hire a nurse for 24-7 to take care of her at home. A couple of times, she was so sick that we had to take her to the hospital, the next to last time was some 3 months before she passed on when she underwent surgery.

That was perhaps my fault; she was very sick and was taken to the hospital. The doctor said that her large intestine was damaged, and if surgery would be done, her survival would be 40%. And the surgeon did not want to do surgery to repair the gut. I said survival would be 0% if surgery would not be done, right? So let us do the surgery. And the surgeon did it, and Marilyn survived and went home; thanks be to the Lord and the surgeon! Her small intestine now ended with a hole in her belly where a bag to catch the feces was located. She went home, and we already had 24-7 nursing aide helpers to take care of her. So she existed like this for about 3 months when her intestinal tract got blocked somehow again, and she fell asleep without waking up or eating for 3 days.

The nurse visited her and assured us that everything was fine. On the 3rd day of such situation, I called the fire department's ambulance, which took her to the hospital; this was November 19, 2020 morning. The nurse followed her and stayed with her in the emergency room while the staff worked on her. They said we could go home and they would call us when she would be taken to her room. In the evening, the hospital called and said they could not do anything, and we should come there. When we got there, she was still sleeping, and the staff said that she was on a ventilator apparatus and nothing could be done to save her. They wanted to take her off away the ventilator apparatus. Alex and I talked and decided to let her go. The apparatus was taken away, and 5 minutes later, at 12:30 AM of November 20, she stopped breathing and passed away. The Lord had taken her soul to his Domain. I called our funeral director, and they took her body to their domain.

Rest in peace, dear Marilyn, and we will be seeing you later, as the Lord will determine. Marilyn's funeral was on November 29, 2020, God bless her soul!

Marilyn's retirement cake.

Marilyn with Father Sergey

Marilyn with Father Sergey and Mrs. Tikoff.

Marilyn with a fellow teacher

3-9

3-10

3-11
13 6 '00

3-11

3-15

3-16

3-18
Москва. Храм Христа Спасителя

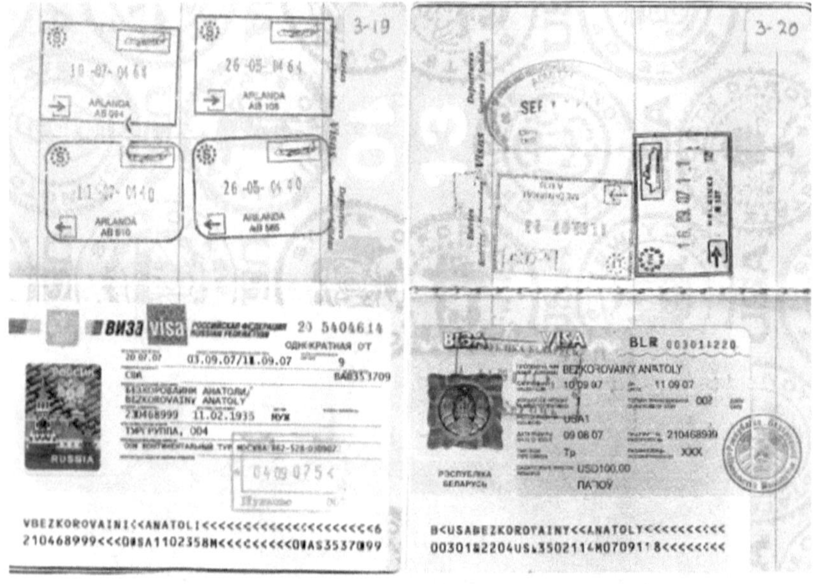

3-21

3-22

3-23

3-24

TRI-STATE
TROLLEY
17
3-25

PARKING
SUPPORT
DUCKS
UNLIMITED
ALENA
ROTARY
3-26

3-27

3-28

3-29

3-31

3-30
WELCOME

3-33

3-37

3-39

3-40

3-41
SPIRIT OF DUBUQUE

DUBUQUE COURT HOUSE

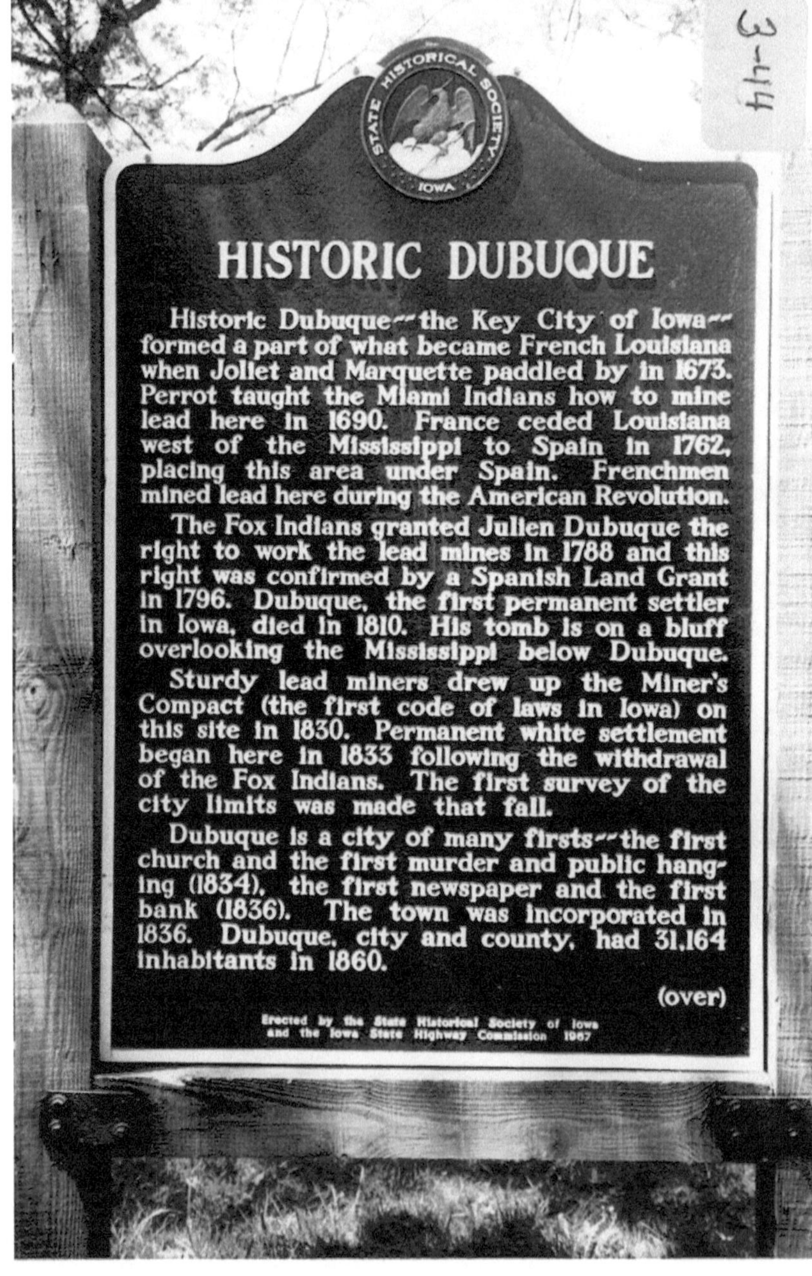
STATE HISTORICAL SOCIETY
IOWA

HISTORIC DUBUQUE

Historic Dubuque--the Key City of Iowa--
formed a part of what became French Louisiana
when Joliet and Marquette paddled by in 1673.
Perrot taught the Miami Indians how to mine
lead here in 1690. France ceded Louisiana
west of the Mississippi to Spain in 1762,
placing this area under Spain. Frenchmen
mined lead here during the American Revolution.

The Fox Indians granted Julien Dubuque the
right to work the lead mines in 1788 and this
right was confirmed by a Spanish Land Grant
in 1796. Dubuque, the first permanent settler
in Iowa, died in 1810. His tomb is on a bluff
overlooking the Mississippi below Dubuque.

Sturdy lead miners drew up the Miner's
Compact (the first code of laws in Iowa) on
this site in 1830. Permanent white settlement
began here in 1833 following the withdrawal
of the Fox Indians. The first survey of the
city limits was made that fall.

Dubuque is a city of many firsts--the first
church and the first murder and public hang-
ing (1834), the first newspaper and the first
bank (1836). The town was incorporated in
1836. Dubuque, city and county, had 31,164
inhabitants in 1860.

(over)

Erected by the State Historical Society of Iowa
and the Iowa State Highway Commission 1967

Fenelon Place Elevator Co.

3-47
SWISS REFORMED CEMETERY

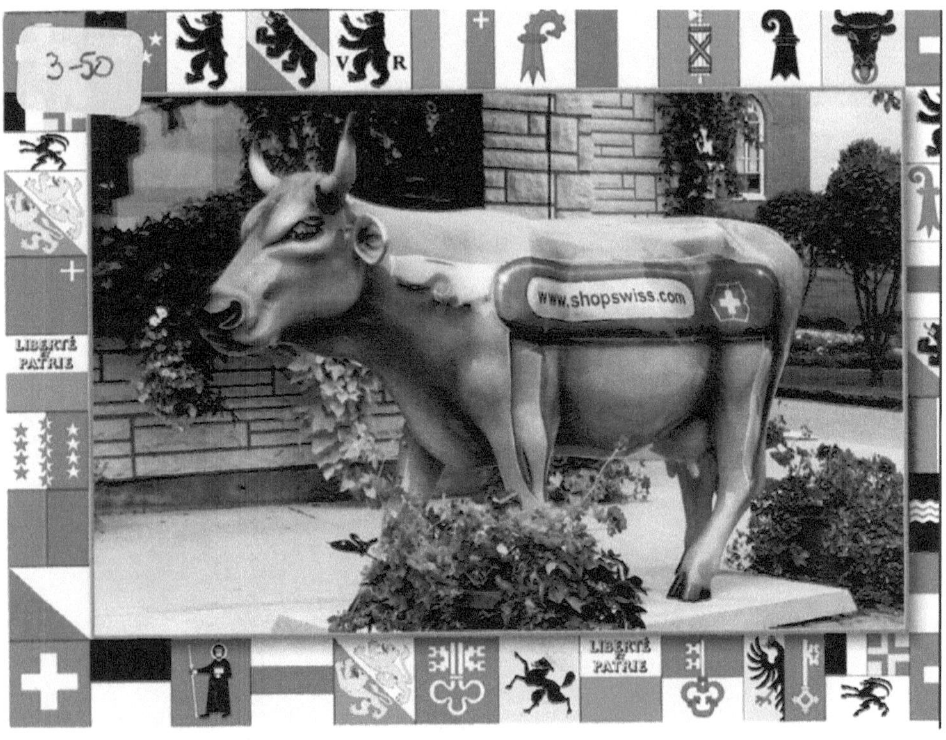
www.shopswiss.com
LIBERTÉ ET PATRIE
LIBERTÉ ET PATRIE
V R

3-51
Roberts
European Imports
Roberts
PHARMACY
EUROPEAN
LIBERTÉ PATRIE
V R
LIBERTÉ PATRIE

3-52

3-53

3-56

3-57

3-101

Home Care Assistance of Scottsdale and Chandler
9301 E Shea Blvd, Ste 112
Scottsdale, AZ 85260
480-499-4944

Client	Bezkorovainy, Marilyn
Invoice No.	16287
Invoice Date	06/01/2020
Date Due	Due upon receipt
From 05/25/2020 **to** 05/31/2020	

Anatoly Bezkorovainy
25449 So. Truro Drive
Sun Lakes, AZ 85248

DESCRIPTION	QUANTITY	RATE	AMOUNT
5/25/20 12:00am - 8:00am Davis, Sherice		450.00/live-in +Holiday	$225
5/25/20 8:00am - 5/26/20 8:00am Davis, Sherice		450.00/live-in +Holiday	$600
5/26/20 8:00am - 5/27/20 8:05am Davis, Sherice		450.00/live-in	$451
5/27/20 8:00am - 5/28/20 8:00am Kapfunde, Olivia		450.00/live-in	$450
5/28/20 8:00am - 5/29/20 7:10am Kapfunde, Olivia		450.00/live-in	$434
5/29/20 7:00am - 8:00am Davis, Sherice		450.00/live-in	$18
5/29/20 8:00am - 5/30/20 8:00am Davis, Sherice		450.00/live-in	$450
5/30/20 8:00am - 5/31/20 8:00am Davis, Sherice		450.00/live-in	$450
5/31/20 8:00am - 11:59pm Davis, Sherice		450.00/live-in	$300

Invoice Total: $3,379.

Marilyn in her casket during her panikhida.

Invoice 16287 - page 2

Last payment(s) received   *Thank you for your payment!*

DATE	DESCRIPTION	AMOUNT
06/01/2020	ACH Settlement	$3,148.44
05/22/2020	ACH Settlement	$3,150.00
05/15/2020	ACH Settlement	$3,154.69
05/11/2020	ACH Settlement	$3,151.57

Aging Summary

CURRENT	1 - 30 DAYS	31 - 60	61 - 90	91+	TOTAL
$0.00	3,379.69	0.00	0.00	0.00	3,379.69

Please tear off this portion and return with your payment to the address below

From:
Anatoly Bezkorovainy
25449 So. Truro Drive
Sun Lakes, AZ 85248

Client: Marilyn Bezkorovainy
Invoice: 16287 - 06/01/2020
Amount Due on This Invoice: $3,379.69
Amount Enclosed: $

Mail to:
Home Care Assistance of Scottsdale a...
9301 E Shea Blvd, Ste 112
Scottsdale, AZ 85260

Egyptian pharaonic monument

Originator of Moscow Art Museum

Russian Holy Trinity Icon

Grave of Father John Garklavs of Chicago

Church of the Greek Orthodox Monastery near Phoenix, Arizona

Orthodox cross at the Greek Orthodox Monastery

Marilyn Bezkorovainy and Dr. Nancy Topouzian, former student of Dr. Anatoly Bezkorovainy

Oldest house in Galena, Illinois built in 1826

Main Street in the city of Galena, Illinois

Bezkorovainy's first house in the Galena Territory with Marilyn looking from behind the car door

One of the original buildings in a town of Wisconsin

The Bezkorovainys with Father and Matushka Sergey Garklavs in the Mississippi River harbor of Dubuque, Iowa

Guests with Mrs. Vera Kijauskas in Scottsdale, AZ (Nora's home): Alexander and Gregory Bezkorovainy and Anatoly Bezkorovainy, Marilyn Bezkorovainy is the photographer

3-115

3-116

3-117